Illustrations by
Giulia De Amicis

THE WORLD of BEES

Text by
Cristina Banfi

WSKids
WHITE STAR KIDS

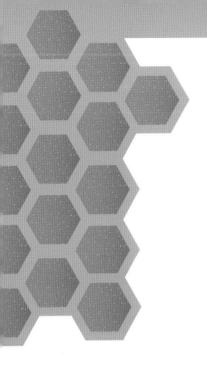

Contents

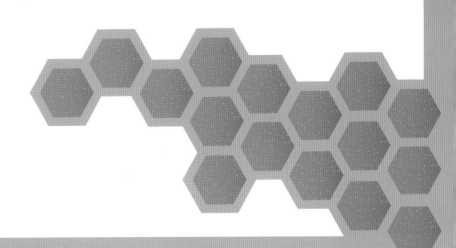

6   Introduction

10   Honey bees

12   Anatomy of a bee

14   Social structure

16   The sense organs

18   Pollination

22   Swarming

24   Communication

26   The bee dance

28   Orientation

30   Bee products

32   The nest

34   The tasks of worker bees

38   Honey-eaters

44   The queen bee's nuptial flight

46   Honey throughout history

52   Between spirituality and symbolism

56   The great bee family

58   Are bees disappearing?

60   Understanding the problem

DO YOU REALLY KNOW BEES?

SURELY YOU KNOW HOW TO RECOGNIZE BEES. You've seen them many times fly on flowers, illustrated in books, or on television, drawn in a funny way in some cartoon. Their yellow and black coloration makes them unique, just like their bad reputation for painful stings...

BUT A BEE IS SO MUCH MORE!

This small insect has a **SECRET LIFE**, full of the most interesting things, like we can't even imagine. To begin with, it lives in a real **KINGDOM**, with a real **QUEEN** that governs her subjects wisely.

WOULD YOU LIKE TO ENTER AND VISIT THEIR EXTRAORDINARY LITTLE WORLD?

This book can take you on a **FANTASTIC JOURNEY** that will bring you directly **INSIDE A BEEHIVE**, to observe the structure of the colony, within which every bee has its own role and carries out a precise task.

WHAT DO YOU DO INSIDE A BEEHIVE?

Here a few **WORKER BEES** are busy taking care of the **QUEEN**, raising **YOUNG LARVAE**, while others are making and storing away the sweet **HONEY**.

But a lot of work is done outside as well: the older and more expert worker bees face the dangers of the world with a lot of courage, going out to seek **POLLEN** and **NECTAR** to bring back to the nest.

EVER WONDER HOW COME THEY NEVER GET LOST?

They possess a special orientation system. Simple, right? You'll be surprised to discover that bees know how to **DANCE**, although they don't do it for fun, but to **COMMUNICATE**. That's right. With rhythmic movements of their body they can "explain" to their fellow bees how far to fly and how to reach a tree full of flowers.

IF YOU PAY CLOSE ATTENTION, YOU TOO WILL BE ABLE TO LEARN THEIR LANGUAGE.

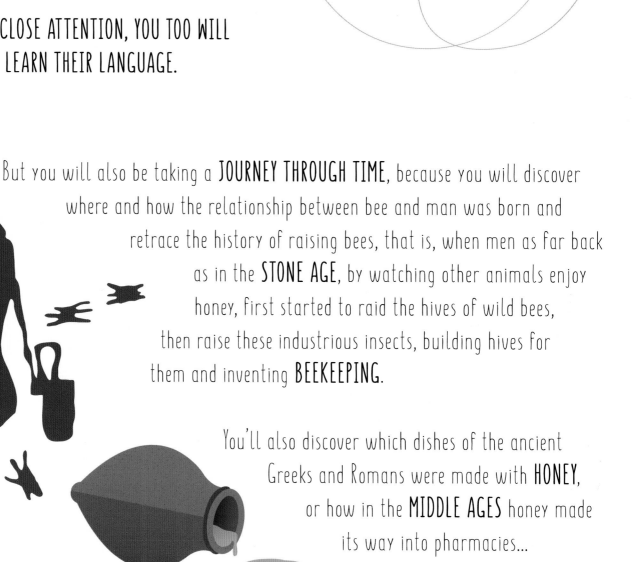

But you will also be taking a **JOURNEY THROUGH TIME**, because you will discover where and how the relationship between bee and man was born and retrace the history of raising bees, that is, when men as far back as in the **STONE AGE**, by watching other animals enjoy honey, first started to raid the hives of wild bees, then raise these industrious insects, building hives for them and inventing **BEEKEEPING**.

You'll also discover which dishes of the ancient Greeks and Romans were made with **HONEY**, or how in the **MIDDLE AGES** honey made its way into pharmacies...

By getting to know bees better, you will realize that they are **PRECIOUS INSECTS**, not only for the products they have to offer, but also because their work is useful for the **ENTIRE PLANET**. Just think...without bees we wouldn't be able to enjoy peaches, apricots and many other juicy fruits...

AND YET, THESE LITTLE FRIENDS TODAY ARE IN DANGER! WHAT IS THREATENING THEM?

All the information in this book on bees will allow you not only to gain a profound knowledge of them, but it will also teach you to **PROTECT** and **HELP** them.
HOW?
First of all, by respecting them, but also by, for example,
**USING YOUR BALCONY OR YOUR GARDEN
IN A "CREATIVE" WAY!**

ENJOY YOUR
READING!

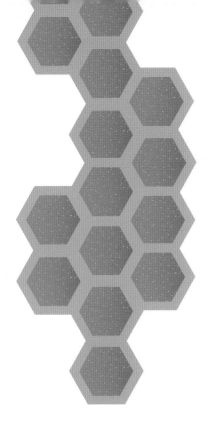

1. HONEY BEES

Everybody knows what bees are, those small yellow and black striped insects that, buzzing, fly from flower to flower. Of course, their sting can be dreadful, but let's not forget that it's only thanks to bees that we can enjoy that sweet and nutritious food: honey.

HOW DID BEES EVOLVE?

Scientists say that they descended from some hunting wasps that changed the source of their diet, switching from being carnivorous to eating nectar.

According to studies of paleontologists, we know that bees made their appearance on Earth together with flowering plants, that is, about 146-74 million years ago, in the course of the geological era called Cretaceous (the last era in which dinosaurs lived).

The oldest fossil bee known to date is of the species *Trigona prisca* and it lived more than 60 million years ago. Its fossil remains have been found in the United States: this species was stingless and, today, is found in many of the tropical and subtropical regions of our planet.

The European honey bee (or *Apis mellifera*), instead, made its appearance more recently, at the end of the Tertiary (about 2 million years ago), but is today the most widespread in the world with 26 subspecies selected by man.

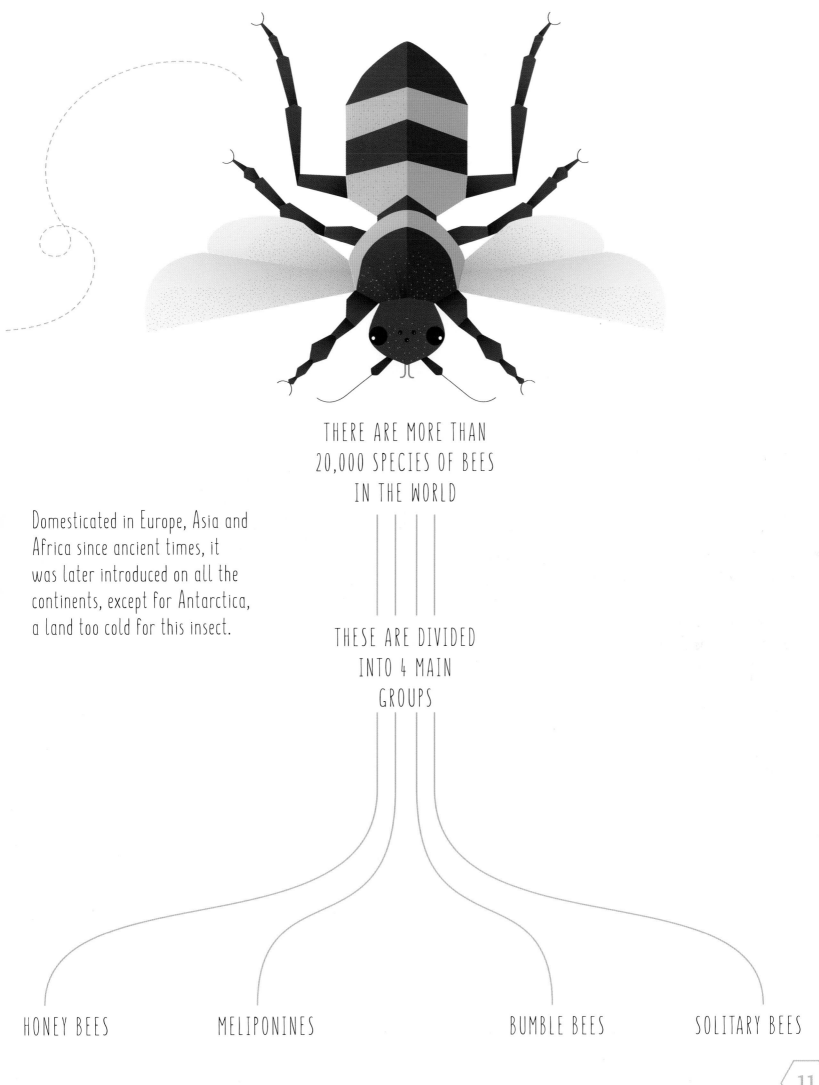

THERE ARE MORE THAN
20,000 SPECIES OF BEES
IN THE WORLD

Domesticated in Europe, Asia and
Africa since ancient times, it
was later introduced on all the
continents, except for Antarctica,
a land too cold for this insect.

THESE ARE DIVIDED
INTO 4 MAIN
GROUPS

HONEY BEES   MELIPONINES   BUMBLE BEES   SOLITARY BEES

2. ANATOMY OF A BEE

Like all insects, bees have a body divided into three sections: head, thorax, and abdomen. Located on the head, besides the mouth, are the sense organs, such as the eyes and the antennae; the organs for movement, instead, are located on the thorax: six legs, just like all the other insects, and four wings. Finally, on the extremity of the abdomen there is a stylet-like structure, the stinger, that, being connected to a venom gland, represents an effective weapon for self-defense and assault.

① HEAD: organs of sense

② THORAX: organs for movement

③ ABDOMEN: organs of defense

Wings

Antennae

Eyes

Stinger

Pollen basket

Legs

THE STINGER

As previously mentioned, though, not all species of bees have stingers: the Meliponine, normally raised in South America and of which 500 species grouped under the name Meliponini are known, is stingless. The Maya people already knew and appreciated its sweet honey, which they called the food of the Gods.

COLORATION

Even the yellow and black striped coloration isn't common to all bees: many, like the violet carpenter bee *Xylocopa violacea*, are even black. On the other hand, not all insects with this type of coloration are bees: wasps and hornets, for example, belong to a completely different family, the Vespidae. There are also harmless flies, the Syrphid flies, that use these colors to imitate bees and wasps and take advantage of the resemblance to trick predators into thinking they are indigestible because of their venom.

Violet carpenter bee
25-30 mm

Honey bee
6-10 mm

APIDAE

Vespa vulgaris
15-20 mm

Vespa crabro
25-35 mm

VESPIDAE

Xanthogramma festivum
8-10 mm

Volucella zonaria
25 mm

SYRPHIDAE

3. SOCIAL STRUCTURE

Many bees, among which the well-known honey bee, are social insects, that is, they live in communities and share the same nest, called hive. Within the group there exists a strict subdivision of tasks and each member works for the well-being of all.

As with other social insects such as ants and termites, the different roles within the bee colony correspond to a different body structure as well.

① THE QUEEN

She is the largest. She lays the eggs and therefore is the mother of all the bees in the hive; she coordinates the work within the group. She has a rather long life, approximately 4 years.

② THE WORKER BEES

They carry out all the tasks necessary to sustain the colony, from taking care of the larvae, to building and defending the hive, to gathering and producing food. In the warmer months of the year their life is quite short, no longer than a month, while those born at the end of summer spend all the winter months with the queen.

③ THE DRONES

These are the male bees and are born from unfertilized eggs. They are slightly larger than worker bees, but are smaller than the queen. Their job is to impregnate the queen during the nuptial flight. Their life is quite short. During the summer their presence is tolerated in the hive, but those still there when winter arrives are harshly driven out and left to die of cold and hunger.

4. THE SENSE ORGANS

Bees, like all insects, perceive the environment that surrounds them differently from how we do and this depends on the sense organs that they possess, which function differently from ours.

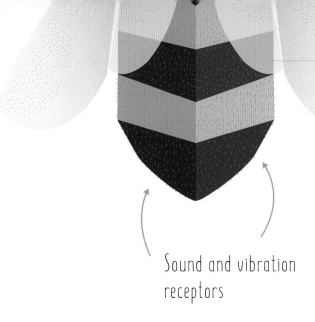

Sound and vibration receptors

TASTE

The receptors involved in tasting food are located on the antennae. Thanks to these, the bee recognizes if something tastes sweet, bitter, salty or acid. If the bee likes what it tastes, then it will extend from its mouth a sort of proboscis and begin to suck.

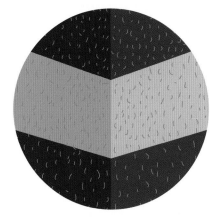

TOUCH

The touch receptors are located on the antennae as well. In fact, bees use them to measure the beehive's cells and keep in touch with their companions by feeling the vibrations of their bodies.

SMELL

Like many insects, bees too produce chemical substances, called pheromones, that spread in the air even to great distances. Picking up the pheromones allows bees to communicate among themselves and recognize strangers in the hive. Since bees do not have a nose, the antennae, on which specific receptors are found, serve to this purpose as well.

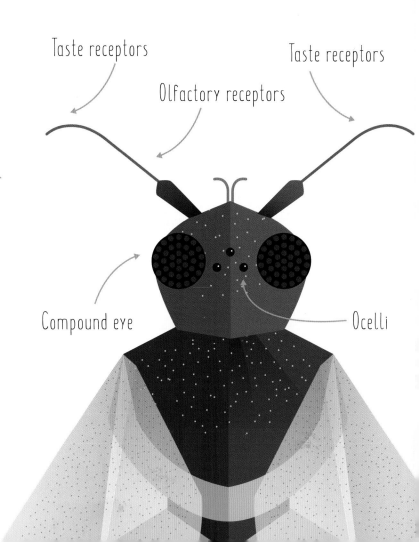

Taste receptors

Taste receptors

Olfactory receptors

Compound eye

Ocelli

HEARING

Bees do not possess ears, yet they can hear sounds thanks to the vibrations that they propagate through the air. These vibrations are intercepted by very sensitive hairs that cover entirely the surface of their body.

SIGHT

Unlike ours, the eyes of bees are compound eyes. Each one has thousands of single receptors of light, and this makes their vision of the world composed of images divided into many single points, in a way similar to a television screen. Furthermore, bees see a color spectrum that is different from the one we see: they can't distinguish well the color red, but they perceive a color invisible to our eye, ultraviolet.

On the head of bees are located three more additional eyes, called ocelli. These eyes don't see colors: they can distinguish only darkness from light and are important organs, especially for orientation. Thanks to particular experiments, some researchers were able to prove that bees can distinguish colors only at a maximum speed of 5 km/hour. At higher speed, their vision of the world is instead black and white.

What a yellow flower looks like to man.

What the same flower looks like to a bee.

5. POLLINATION

Pollination is the process that enables plants to be fertilized. Pollen from one flower unites with the egg cell of another flower and fecundates it, giving origin to the fruit that will contain the seeds necessary for the birth of new generations of plants, guaranteeing the continuity of the species.

To transfer the pollen, some plants rely on the wind, others on water, and many count on animals, particularly insects, that, while feeding on the sweet nectar, involuntarily gather the pollen and distribute it among the various flowers that they visit, one after the other.

In time, plants have evolved incredible stratagems to attract insects, beginning with the scent and the colors, often brilliant, of their flowers. Bees love particularly the colors yellow and blue, while they can't see at all the color red.

As we know, they can see ultraviolet light: on many flowers whose appearance may seem insignificant to us, there are stripes of pigments, invisible to our eyes, that reflect this light and that represent an irresistible attraction for bees. They represent, in fact, a sign that makes them recognizable as a source of nectar and that sends a clear message to insects:

"Come over here, we're the perfect place to visit!".

We must never forget that the majority of crop yield in agriculture, in gardening, and in orchards depends on bee pollination.

It is estimated that about a third of the vegetables that man consumes is pollinated by bees: zucchini, bean and pea plants, as well as many fruit trees such as apple, pear, apricot, peach and almonds trees, and also strawberries, blueberries and raspberries need bees to produce their delicious fruits.

PLANTS THAT DEPEND ON BEE POLLINATION

The methods employed by bees to gather pollen are diverse: in some species it remains trapped in the hairs that cover their body; in others, such as honey bees, little baskets called corbiculae are located on the legs and in these pollen is accumulated, so as to be more easily transported.

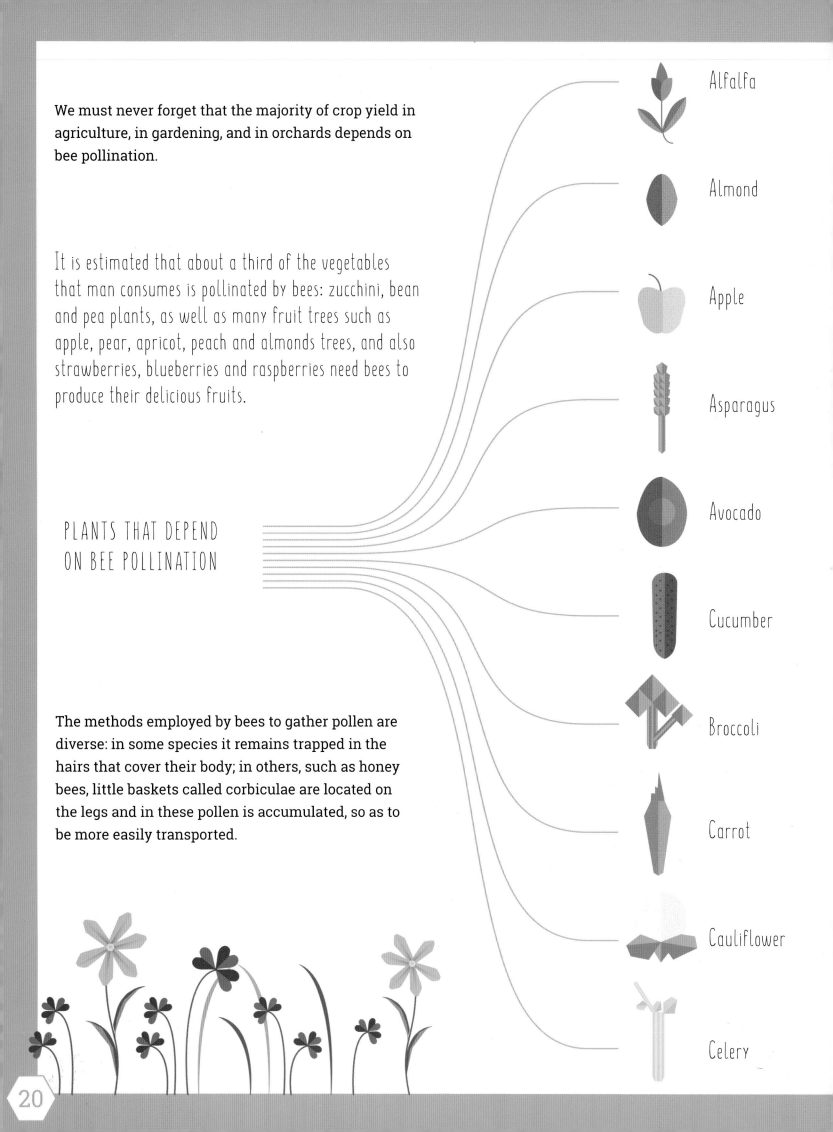

Alfalfa

Almond

Apple

Asparagus

Avocado

Cucumber

Broccoli

Carrot

Cauliflower

Celery

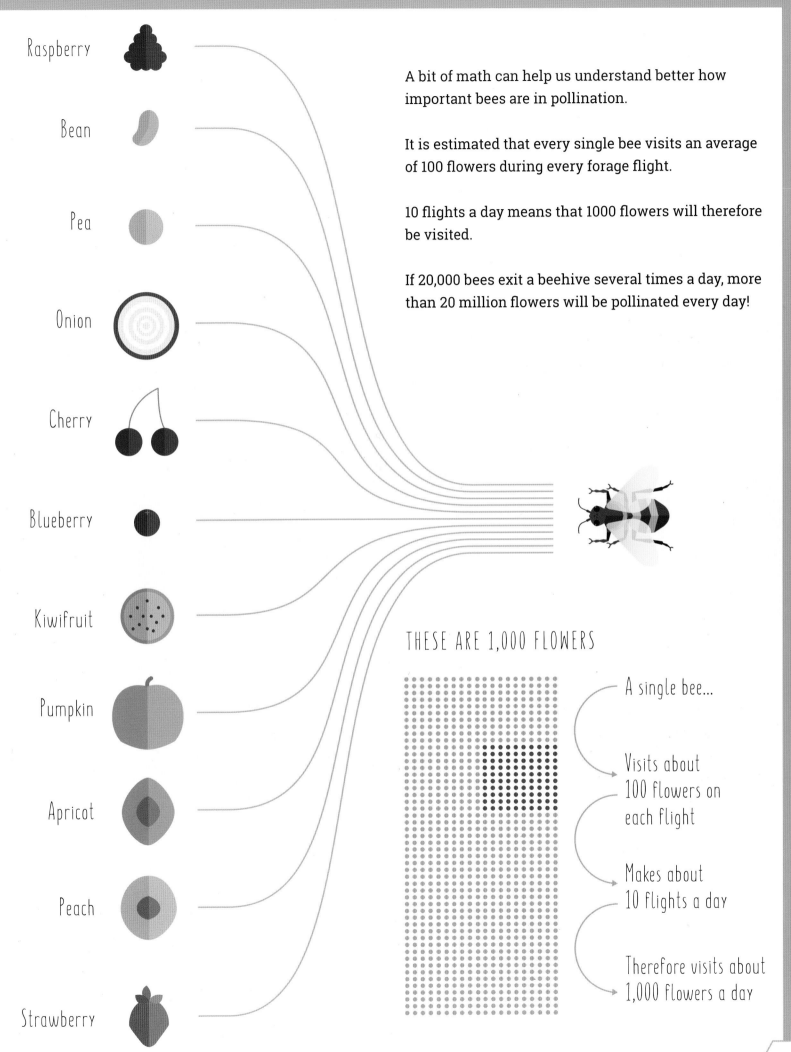

Raspberry

Bean

Pea

Onion

Cherry

Blueberry

Kiwifruit

Pumpkin

Apricot

Peach

Strawberry

A bit of math can help us understand better how important bees are in pollination.

It is estimated that every single bee visits an average of 100 flowers during every forage flight.

10 flights a day means that 1000 flowers will therefore be visited.

If 20,000 bees exit a beehive several times a day, more than 20 million flowers will be pollinated every day!

THESE ARE 1,000 FLOWERS

A single bee...

Visits about 100 flowers on each flight

Makes about 10 flights a day

Therefore visits about 1,000 flowers a day

6. SWARMING

There comes the day when, in the beehive, the old queen decides that the moment has arrived to create another colony, taking a part of its daughters elsewhere. The group of worker bees that will leave the hive is called swarm and its transferal to colonize other places is therefore called swarming.

Swarming is the means by which bees can originate new colonies, especially when the beehive becomes overpopulated. For many wild bees, though, swarming is also a means to colonize other geographical regions in search of food, or to move the beehive from a place that is no longer safe. In this case, swarming, which normally takes place in the warmer months, can take place even in the middle of winter.

The queen coordinates the pre-departure activities: the swarming bees gather a sufficient amount of honey to be sure to have 5 or 6 days' worth of food supplies, and are laden to the point of being unable to extract their stinger: this is why bees seldom sting during swarming.

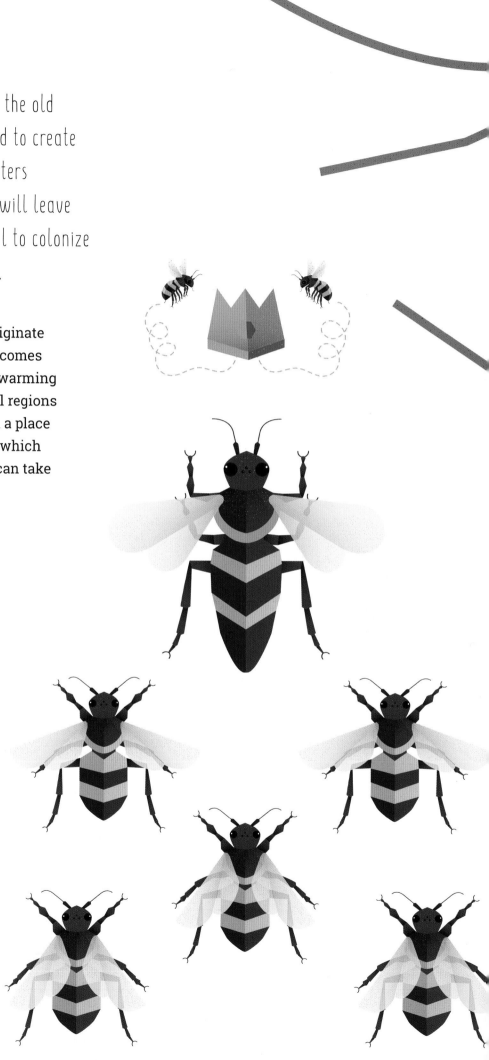

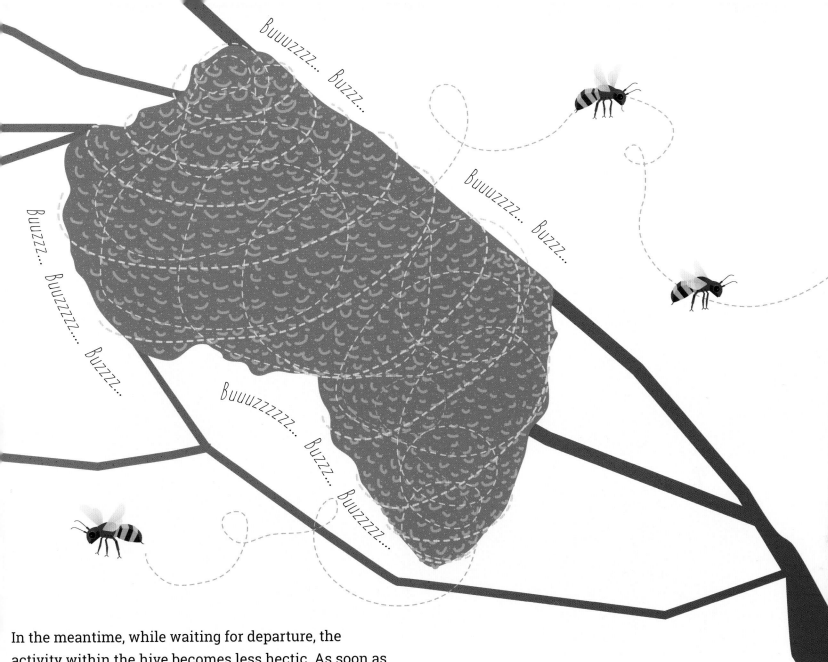

In the meantime, while waiting for departure, the activity within the hive becomes less hectic. As soon as everything is ready, the old queen gathers a few thousand worker bees and leads them outside the beehive.

The bees arrange themselves around the queen in order to protect her from possible predators. They can even make intermediate stops in temporary locations, forming those characteristic clusters that remain 2-3 days hanging down from tree branches or rock protrusions.

Within the mass of bodies lies the queen, surrounded by the younger bees. Arranged on the outer side are the older and more expert bees who, taking turns, leave the group and scout the surroundings in search of the best place to build the new nest.

In the old colony, meanwhile, arrangements have already been made to give birth to and raise a new queen, who will begin to lay eggs, taking the place of the older one that has flown away.

7. COMMUNICATION

Living within a group, which can consist of many individuals, means knowing how to follow precise community rules and, above all, possessing a system that enables a good coordination between members of the same species. It is therefore necessary for them to share the same communication system, and this holds true for bees as well.

To do this, besides using those special "odors" called pheromones, bees have developed a complex system of communication, truly unique among insects, that involves body movements.

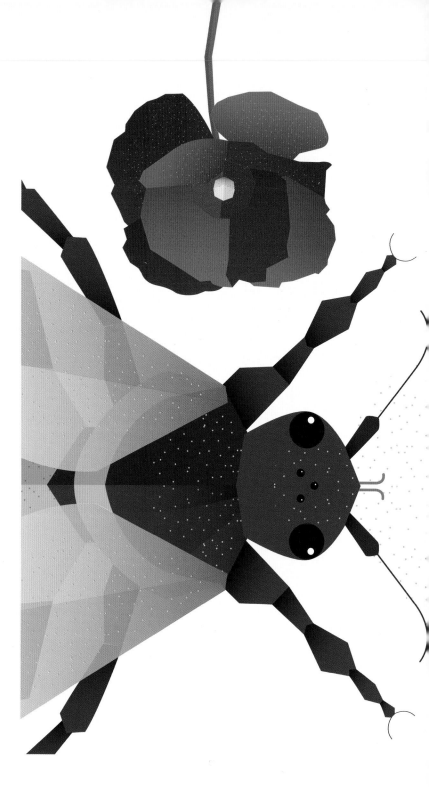

Bees, during their flights to scout the area and gather pollen, can wander even several miles away from their hive in search of rich and easily accessible sources of food, such as a lawn or a tree in full bloom.

When they find one, upon returning to the beehive they perform a special "dance". This is their way of sharing the precious information with the other bees in the hive.

By performing a precise sequence of rhythmic movements with the abdomen, accompanied by a certain inclination of the body, the bee is capable of giving instructions with extreme precision as to where the place to go is and exactly how far it lies from the beehive.

Furthermore, using their antennae to smell the pollen left on the bee's body, the other bees can also identify what type of plant they must try to find.

It wasn't easy for zoologists to decipher this unique "language": it was the Austrian naturalist Karl von Frisch, an animal behavior researcher, who succeeded after about 20 years of studies and observations.

The pollen left on the antennae tells the bees which flower to look for.

For his long and valuable work, Von Frisch won the Nobel Prize in Physiology or Medicine. He recognized two types of movements: the circular dance and the waggle dance.

8. THE BEE DANCE

When they return from their foraging flights, bees start to twirl around near the entrance to the beehive, then they enter, lean against a wall and here they start to walk, making circular movements among the other bees who are present at the "dance".

WHAT'S HAPPENING?

The movements the dancing bee performs are not at all random. Instead, they enable the bee to transmit a message: having found food for the colony, it is in fact recruiting co-workers to help gather it. They all have to observe very carefully because it is telling them where to go.

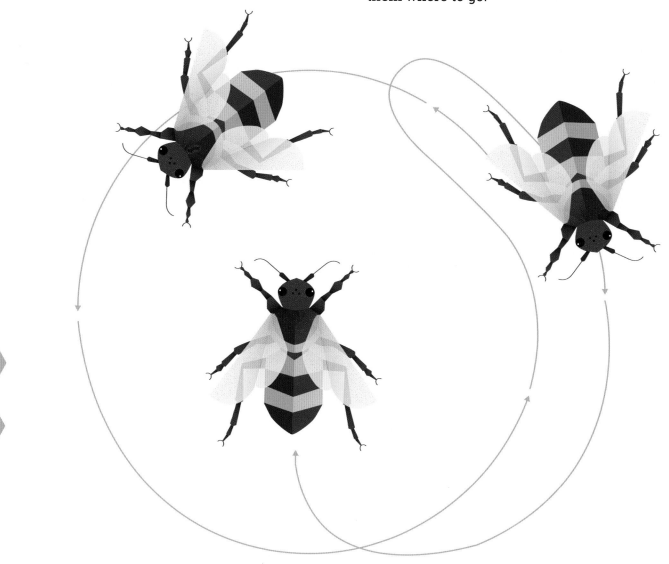

The dance must be understood in the following manner: if the source of food is located at less than 164 feet (50 m) from the beehive, the bee walks in circles, going first one way and then the other. This signal will make the companions take off and, by moving in ever wider circles, they will find the place indicated.

CIRCULAR DANCE

Source of food at less than 164 feet (50 m)

If, instead, the place to go is further away, the bee modifies its dance: the walk becomes a figure-eight pattern, by covering a short distance in a straight line, then performing a 360°-turn, first right and then left. In doing this, the bee vibrates its abdomen in intervals. The speed at which it completes these steps and the number of vibrations of its abdomen in the unit of time indicate at what distance the source of food is to be found. The slower the speed of movement, the further away the bees will have to go.

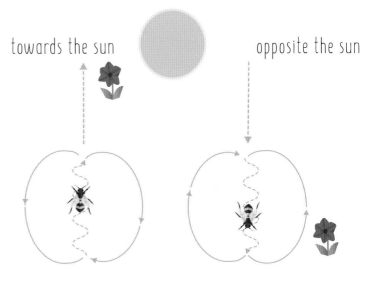

towards the sun   opposite the sun

Even the sun, along with the force of gravity, represents a reference point for the bees: if the dancing bee directs the linear steps of its dance upwards, it means that the source of food is located in the same direction as the sun; if, instead, they are directed downward, the source of food will have to be sought after in the opposite direction.

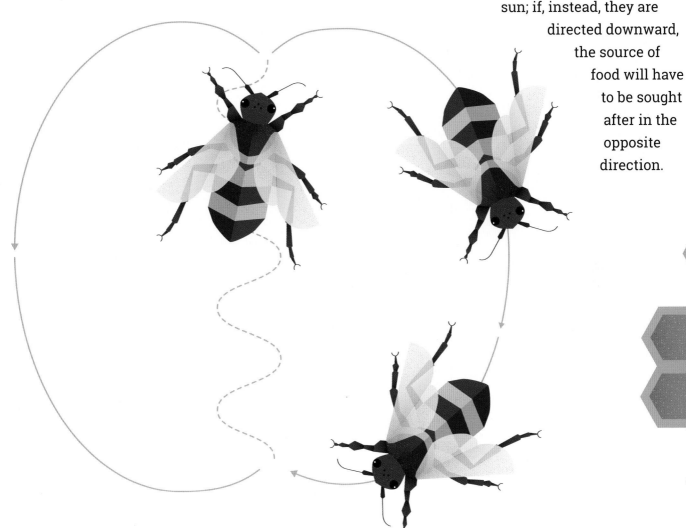

Additionally, if the circle is set at a certain angle, the bee is communicating to the others that they have to fly to the right or to the left of the sun, following a trajectory that must have the same angle as the one shown during the dance, on the right or left of an imaginary line.

WAGGLE DANCE

Source of food at more than 164 feet (50 m)

9. ORIENTATION

Bees, during their exploration flights in search of nectar, always manage to find their way home. How come they never get lost?

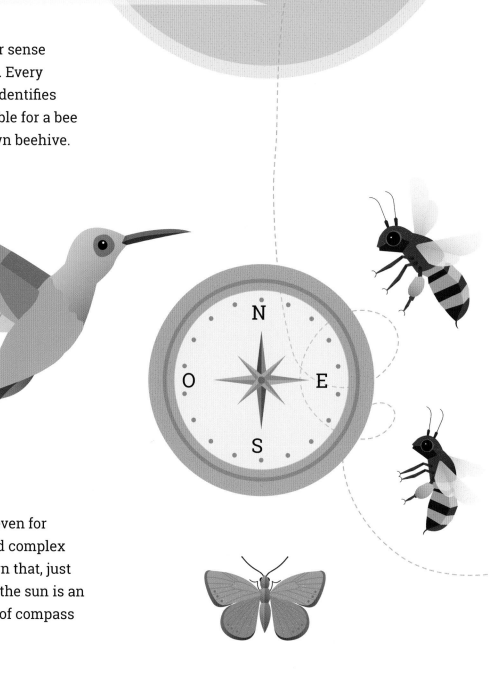

If the distance is short, surely they use their sense of sight, and especially their sense of smell. Every bee family has its own peculiar smell that identifies it precisely, so that it is practically impossible for a bee to make the mistake of entering an unknown beehive.

The Sun represents an important tool for the orientation of bees, butterflies and birds.

Bees, though, can fly away from their nest even for several miles, often covering non-linear and complex routes. For years now, scientists have known that, just as for birds and butterflies, for bees as well the sun is an important instrument of orientation, a sort of compass for navigation.

Even when the sky is cloudy, bees sense the light that filters through the clouds: the way in which it reaches their eyes provides a clear clue as to the position of the sun in the sky, even if it's not visible.

Recently, some scientific studies have suggested that bees can even create actual mental maps, like mammals do, memorizing the reference points they see in their surroundings.

A curious experiment was performed: after having selected a few bees from a beehive, their day/night rhythm was modified so that they wouldn't be able to figure out what moment of the day it was, not even by observing the Sun's position in the sky. The scientists noticed that these "confused" bees could actually return to the beehive with no problem at all, just like their sisters. These studies show that, clearly, even remembering the position of a bush, a rock, or a building allows bees to calculate the distance between these reference points and the beehive, without having to resort to the Sun. This ability is so much more surprising if we think how small a brain these insects possess.

10. BEE PRODUCTS

Since ancient times, man knows and values the precious products of bees. In fact, to have them always available, he has learned to raise these hard-working insects that, in turn, appreciate the protection that domestic life offers.

HONEY

It's the main nourishment of bees, which they make starting from nectar and from honeydew, another sugary substance gathered from plants. Bees store it in the little honeycomb cells, sealing them afterwards. It is used, in case of necessity, to feed the members of the colony. This is why it's important, when man gathers it for human use, that there always be left a sufficient amount to nourish the bees, especially during the colder months. Honey is 85% sugar (fructose and glucose), so, besides tasting good, it is highly energetic and rich in vitamins.

ROYAL JELLY

It's the gelatinous food with which the larvae destined to be queens are nourished. It is derived from the processing of pollen and mixed with a particular fluid produced by glands located on the head of nurse bees. Royal jelly represents a nutriment rich in protein and vitamins, has a white color and a taste that is between acid and sweet. Man uses it as a remedy against physical weakness following illness or fatigue.

WAX

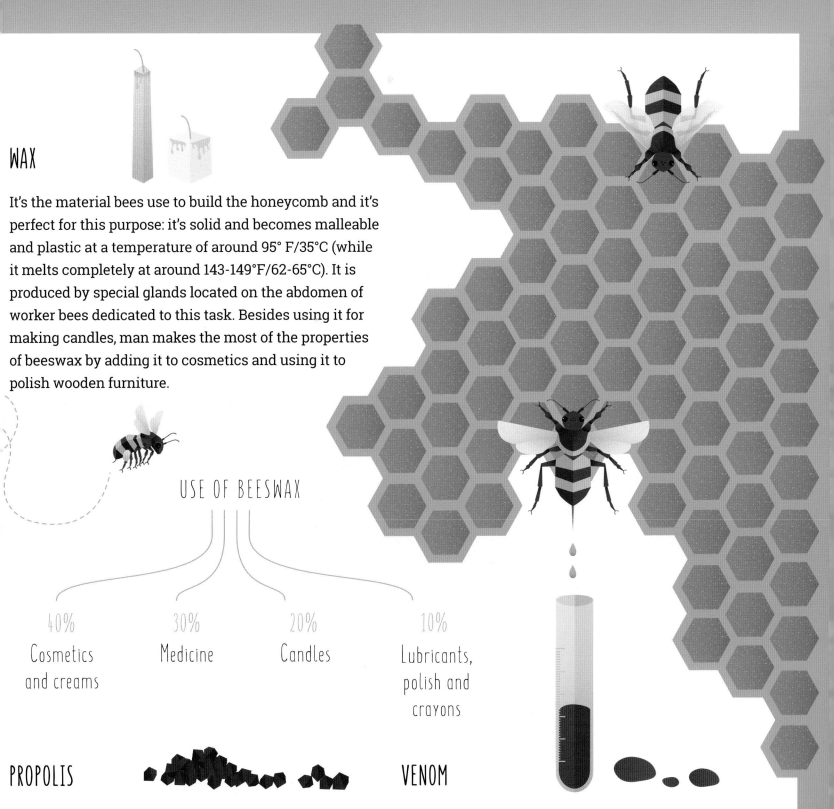

It's the material bees use to build the honeycomb and it's perfect for this purpose: it's solid and becomes malleable and plastic at a temperature of around 95° F/35°C (while it melts completely at around 143-149°F/62-65°C). It is produced by special glands located on the abdomen of worker bees dedicated to this task. Besides using it for making candles, man makes the most of the properties of beeswax by adding it to cosmetics and using it to polish wooden furniture.

USE OF BEESWAX

40%	30%	20%	10%
Cosmetics and creams	Medicine	Candles	Lubricants, polish and crayons

PROPOLIS

It's a powerful antibacterial that bees produce from the resins gathered off the bark of trees such as poplars, oaks, conifers, after having processed and pre-digested it. It is sticky and dark red in color. Propolis is used by bees to disinfect; it is spread on the walls of the beehive and on the dead bodies of casual intruders too big to be carried out of the nest. It is used by man for its antibiotic and anti-inflammatory properties.

VENOM

It's the substance bees use the most for self-defense, injecting it in their assailants through their sting. If a bee stings us, it is destined to die because the stinger is barbed and remains stuck in our skin; in attempting to fly away, the bee tears its intestines. This doesn't happen though if it stings another insect. The bee's venom is gathered and used by man for its numerous therapeutic properties, in particular, it's an excellent remedy against rheumatisms, and it contrasts certain diseases of the nervous system.

11. THE NEST

Wild bees that live in colonies build their common nest in a place that is safe and dry, sheltered and protected by the branches of a tree or in the crack of a rocky mountain side. Inside, small hexagonal wax cells are built, with the opening slightly turned upwards, fit for containing the larvae during the stage of development or to store supplies of pollen and honey.

The inside of the honey bee nest

THE NEST OF HONEY BEES

The hexagonal form of the cells isn't casual; in fact, it represents the shape that best ensures solidity of the structure and room for containing and storing, while using the least amount of wax possible. The numerous continuously joined cells make up the honeycomb. The beekeeper prepares the outer structure or hive artificially, making the bees' work easier.

THE NEST OF MINING BEES

Among the solitary wild bees, "mining bees" are very common; they build their own nest underground, digging a tunnel with their jaws and using their legs to carry the crumbled dirt to the surface. They often build small heaps of dirt at the entrance, arranged so as to prevent rain from entering.

The cells of the nest containing larvae

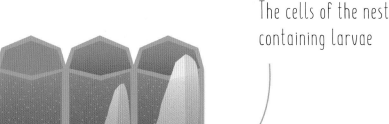

Mining bee

THE NEST OF BUILDER BEES

Other bees, instead, are called "builders" because, taking advantage of already existing natural cavities, such as crevices in rocks, tree trunks, as well as empty shells, they coat them with natural material such as resin, mud, excrements, or even the pulp of petals, and normally lay several eggs per nest, separating them with partitioning that the bee makes with a mixture of mud, saliva, or with fragments of leaves that the insect itself tears up (such as, for example, *Osmia rufa* and the *Megachilidae* family).

Builder bee

THE NEST OF CARPENTER BEES

Carpenter bees, equipped with powerful jaws, dig their own nest out of wood and lay few very large eggs. Some species keep guard of the offspring until it has fully developed (such as, for example, *Xylocopa violacea*).

At the end of the main tunnel, they prepare the room for the egg, which the bee coats with an insulating substance that she herself makes and, together with the egg, she leaves a supply of nectar and pollen that will serve to nourish the larva that will be born. Once the tunnel is sealed, the bee will build another one for another egg, and so on (e.g. genre *Dasypoda*).

Violet carpenter bee

12. THE TASKS OF WORKER BEES

Worker bees represent almost the entirety of the beehive population. Like the queen, they are all females, but they are sterile. They are smaller, with a shorter abdomen and a sort of tiny basket on their legs, fit for bringing pollen back to the nest. Every day the bees have to carry out an incredible amount of chores and tasks, but they work as a team, with a subdivision of roles and work to do that is closely related to the age of the bee. That is to say that the tasks change during the course of their short life.

1-3 DAYS

As soon as metamorphosis has taken place, the bee's job is to clean the cell from which it came out, along with all the surrounding cells, so as to make them ready to receive new eggs, or to store a supply of honey and pollen.

3-6 DAYS

In the next few days, it keeps the beehive clean, removing any dead bees or larvae and carrying them outside the beehive. Even sick bees are sent away, so that they don't become a threat for the well-being of the entire colony.

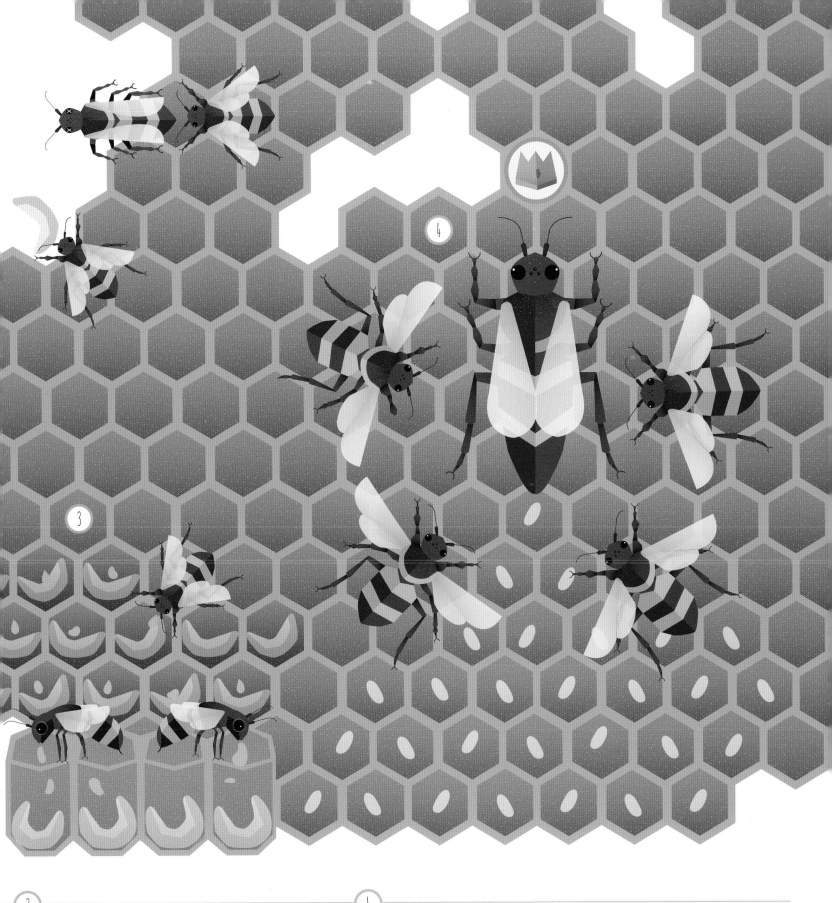

3
6–10 DAYS

After a few days, the young bees become nurses and take care of the developing larvae, nourishing them and constantly checking on them, up to 1,300 times a day.

4
10–12 DAYS

The successive tasks involve caring for the queen bee, taking care of her necessities, such as nourishment and cleaning, and assisting her while she lays in the cells up to 2,000 eggs a day. The "attendant" bees also have to transmit the messages of the queen, that communicates through pheromones, to all their sisters.

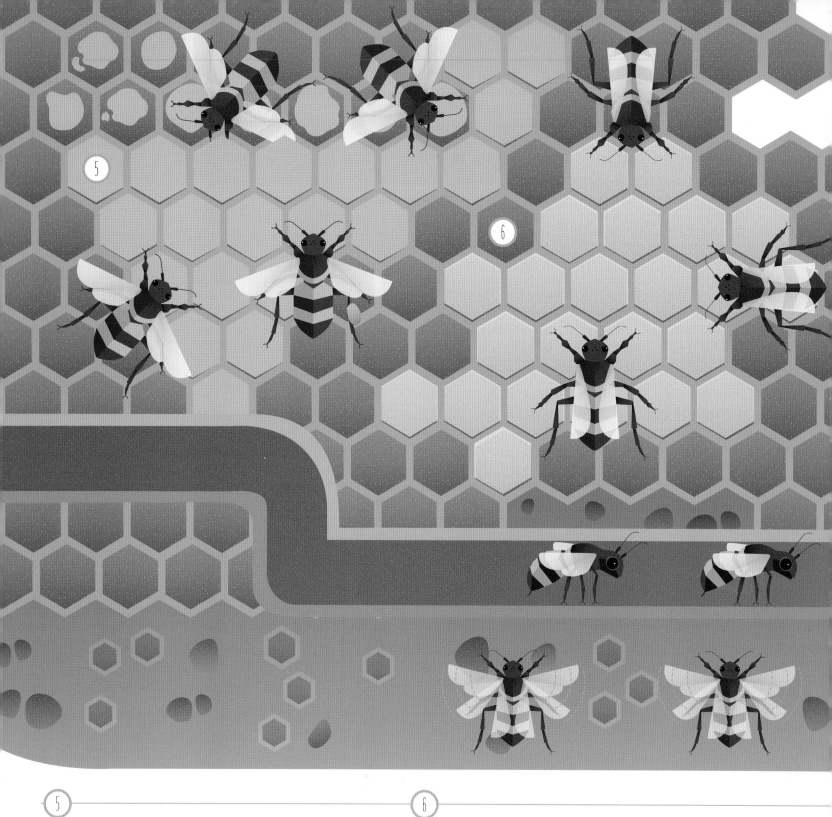

12-16 DAYS

When they are about 12 days old, the young bees receive nectar and pollen from the forager bees when these return to the hive, transform them into honey, and deposit it in the small honeycomb cells destined for storage.

16-20 DAYS

After little more than two weeks, the bees are mature enough to start producing the wax that, being a very plastic material, is used to build the honeycomb's perfectly hexagonal cells, along with the lids, if they are to preserve honey.

Besides all this, bees are busy maintaining the temperature within the beehive as constant as possible and never over 97°F/36°C. Therefore, on the hottest summer days, they use their bodies to shield the brood and create air currents by moving their wings fast. Aside from being required to safeguard the correct and complete development of the larvae, air circulation ensures the ripening of the honey, preventing undesired fermentation.

Instead, in the winter, when the temperature outside drops, bees, which are cold-blooded animals, below 50°F/10°C become inactive and, to survive, they gather together in the areas of the hive where the supplies of honey and pollen are stored. They clump together to form a large ball of bodies. The innermost layers are the warmest, while the outer ones are colder. This is the reason why the bees keep changing place.

Bees are engaged in maintaining a constant temperature in the beehive.

20-23 DAYS

When it is about 20 days old, the bee performs the last household chore: defending the beehive. It stations with its peers, alert and attentive, at the entrance of the nest and ensures that only members of the family pass. Bees with an unfamiliar smell will be sent away, even if occasionally a foreign bee, by corrupting the guardians with some nectar, manages to enter to steal some honey.

23-40 DAYS

About halfway through its life, the worker bee is ready for the hardest and most dangerous task, which will lead it to work outside. In fact, it joins its sister foragers, but only after first going on some quick orientation flights around the hive: these flights have the important purpose of allowing bees to memorize the appearance and the position of their home, the reference points that will guide them back when they will venture to places further and further away.

13. HONEY-EATERS

Humans are not the only ones to have discovered how good and nutritious honey is. Many animals have added this precious food to their diet and, in order to get it, are ready to face the bees and their aggressiveness, accepting the inevitable painful stings that they inflict on those who plunder their nests.

HABITUAL AND CASUAL PREDATORS

Some, like the badger or the fox, are casual predators, while others have physical characteristics or have developed special behavioral techniques in order to be able to regularly feed on the sweet honey.

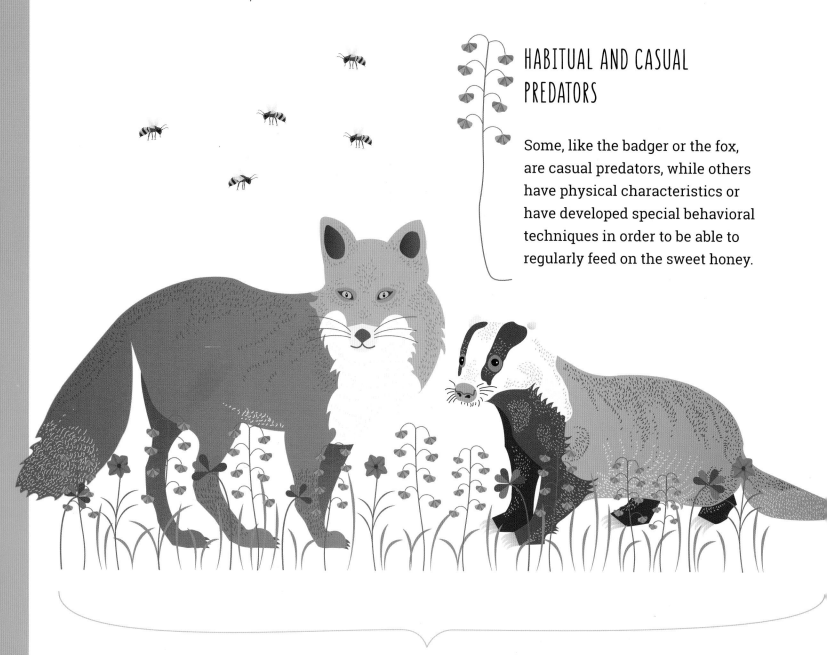

The fox and the badger are casual honey-eaters.

Bears are protected by their thick fur and, thanks to their long claws, can open and destroy a beehive completely, while chimpanzees use thin sticks that they insert into honeycombs and, once they extract them all dripping with honey, suck them as if they were lollypops.

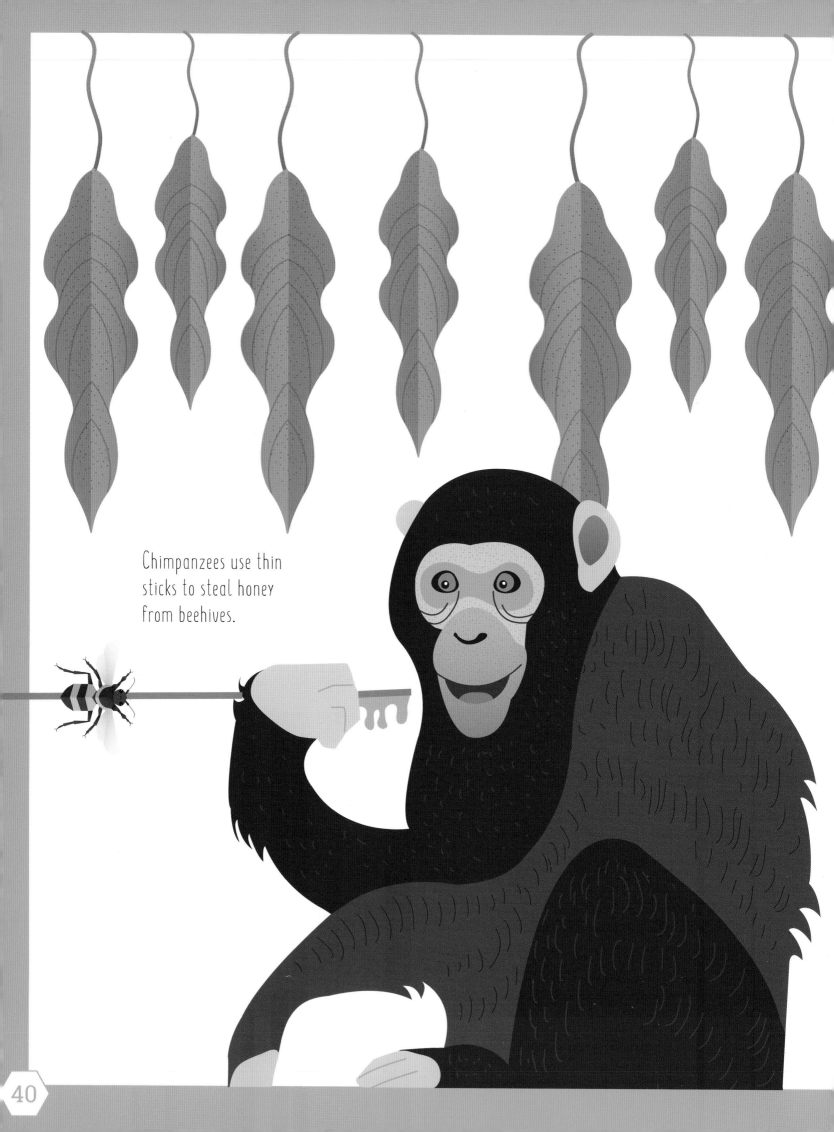

Chimpanzees use thin sticks to steal honey from beehives.

THE HONEY BADGER

Also called Mellivora or ratel, it holds in its name the most obvious of its characteristics: it is a skilled predator of beehives, which it assails frequently to devour honey and larvae.

Its tough skin, rubbery and thick, can resist even the assault of spears and arrows and so it is practically impossible for bee stings to penetrate it, even if they are hundreds.

The honey badger lives in Africa, in the Middle East, and in India.

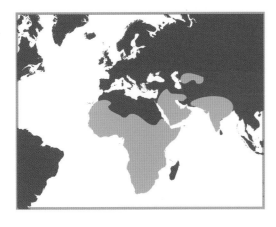

This curious mammal lives in Africa, in the Middle East, and in India and gets its name from the resemblance with the European badger, with which, though, it is unrelated.

"EXTRAORDINARY" PREDATORS

In South America, instead, lives the kinkajou (*Potos flavus*), a small mammal related to raccoons, that moves around on trees and that often, thanks to its prehensile tail, hangs from their branches.

The honey bear lives in Central and South America.

It is also known as honey bear because it uses its long tongue (up to 8 inches/12 cm) to suck honey out of beehives, enrichening its diet with this nutrient.

The kinkajou's tongue can reach 8 inches (12 cm) in length.

The greater wax moth

Even among insects, there are some that fancy the work of bees. An example is the greater wax moth (*Galleria mellonella*), which represents a plague to beehives. It's a nocturnal butterfly that lays eggs in beehives: its caterpillars are greedy wax and honey-eaters and their presence can destroy an entire beehive in no time.

The great *Acherontia atropos* butterfly (or greater death's head hawkmoth) damages bees when it reaches adulthood: thanks to its thick fur and immunity to venom, it endures the attack of the guardian bees and enters the beehive at night to eat the honey.

The greater death's head hawkmoth.

14. THE QUEEN BEE'S NUPTIAL FLIGHT

The bees' larvae are fed for the first three days by royal jelly, then nectar and pollen until their metamorphosis. The larvae destined to be queens, instead, keep eating royal jelly until they develop. At birth, the queen is not yet fertile. To be so, she must first be fecundated.

Mating doesn't take place in the beehive with her colony's drones, but rather outside with those from other hives. To do this, the queen must undertake the nuptial flight, that is, she must momentarily leave her home. This happens about ten days after her metamorphosis on a hot windless day.

After the first few circular orientation flights, the queen bee, accompanied by her servants, which are in charge of protecting her from potential predators, rises up to 65 feet (20 m) in the air. She will be followed by the drones present in that area who have scented her pheromone: this acts as an irresistible signal.

A dozen males will reach her and fecundate her in flight. Multiple matings will allow the queen to collect up to 7 million spermatozoa that she will be able to use to fertilize the eggs she will lay during her entire life.

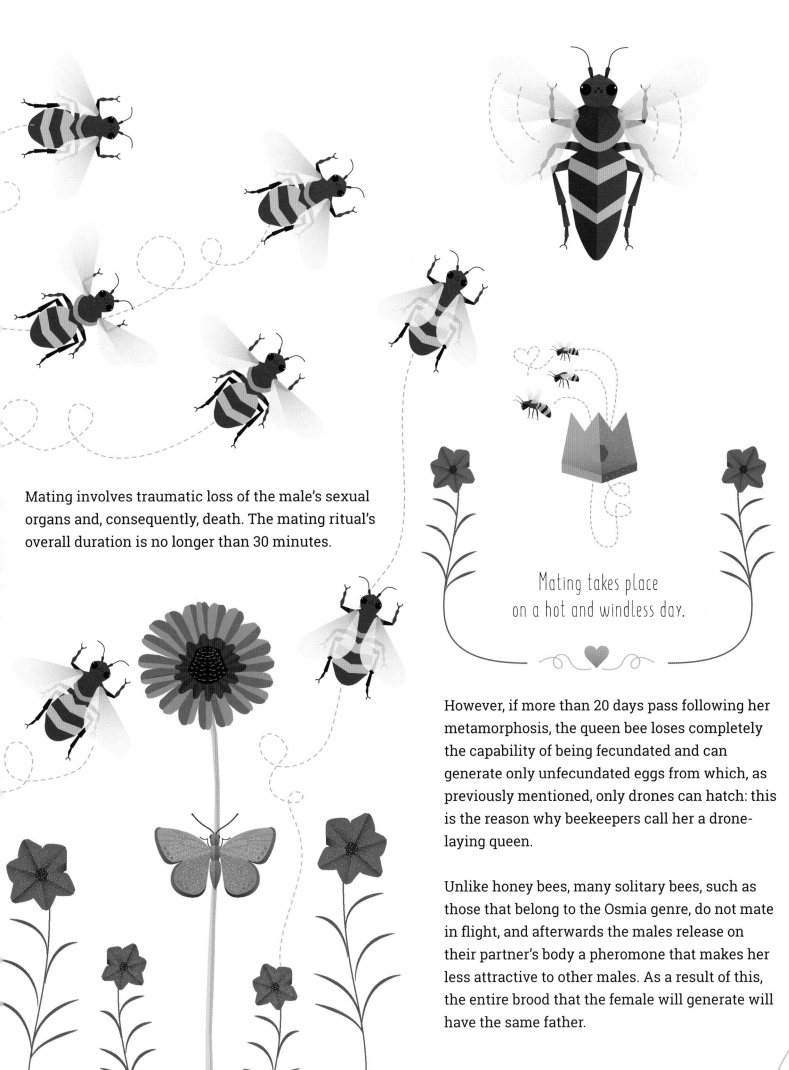

Mating involves traumatic loss of the male's sexual organs and, consequently, death. The mating ritual's overall duration is no longer than 30 minutes.

Mating takes place
on a hot and windless day.

However, if more than 20 days pass following her metamorphosis, the queen bee loses completely the capability of being fecundated and can generate only unfecundated eggs from which, as previously mentioned, only drones can hatch: this is the reason why beekeepers call her a drone-laying queen.

Unlike honey bees, many solitary bees, such as those that belong to the Osmia genre, do not mate in flight, and afterwards the males release on their partner's body a pheromone that makes her less attractive to other males. As a result of this, the entire brood that the female will generate will have the same father.

15. HONEY THROUGHOUT HISTORY

We don't know exactly when man tasted the sweetness of honey for the first time, but surely at least 8,000 years ago, in the Neolithic era, some daring individual was capable of stealing it from the hives of wild bees. It is documented on the walls of Spanish caves, the Cuevas de la Araña (Caves of the Spider), discovered near Valencia.

It is a work of cave art that dates to 5-6,000 years ago, in which the figure of a man on top of a tree is shown. He holds a basket in his hand and many bees are buzzing around him; also shown, some smoke with which he was probably attempting to stun them. He appears to be applying the same technique used today by the "honey hunters" of India.

The Egyptian wild bee

The even older remains of honey have instead been found in Georgia, in clay vases contained in a tomb that dates back about 5,000 years.

The cave art of the Caves of the Spider is located in Spain.

Russia

Turkey

Georgia lies between Turkey and Russia and gives onto the Black Sea.

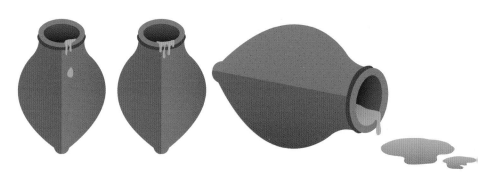

HONEY FOR THE EGYPTIANS: A DIVINE FOOD

The first people to raise bees, though, were the Egyptians: an Egyptian painting found in the Sun Temple, near Cairo, shows us that 2,400 years ago these people used to build horizontal beehives and gather from them the precious substance.

Anubis, the jackal god

Queen Nefertiti

Horus, the falcon god

At the beginning it was reserved for the royal family and the deities, and only afterwards was it consumed by the population as well, who used it to make desserts and cookies.

The kingdom of Egypt at its greatest expansion.

Honey was also used to embalm the dead, to prepare unguents used for curing sores and wounds, as payment of taxes, and as gift to the gods.

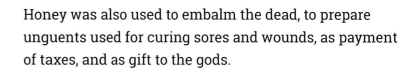

THE WORD "HONEY"

The word seems to have originated from the Germanic branch of the Indo-European word for "golden yellow", *k(e)neko*, later becoming *huna(n)go* in ancient Germanic, then *honung* in Old Norse, and finally *hunig* in Old English.

HONEY IN ANCIENT GREECE

The ancient Greeks showed a vivid interest in beekeeping: even the great philosopher Aristotle described it in his essay *De Generatione Animalium*, and drew up the first original hypotheses on the formation of honey, believing it to fall from the sky.

HONEY FOR THE ANCIENT ROMANS

The Romans too raised bees and built hives for them of different sizes and using different materials, such as wicker, terracotta, bark, and many others. They used honey to sweeten any food, particularly wine, which was otherwise too acid and almost undrinkable. It was also used, though, to preserve food, to make sauces, and to flavor dishes: the ancient Romans, in fact, enjoyed dishes that had a much more sweet-and-sour taste than ours.

Honey was also used in perfumes and as a remedy for wounds, and even to give greater brilliance to the purple color of fabrics. The cost of honey was comparable to that of fine wines and precious oils.

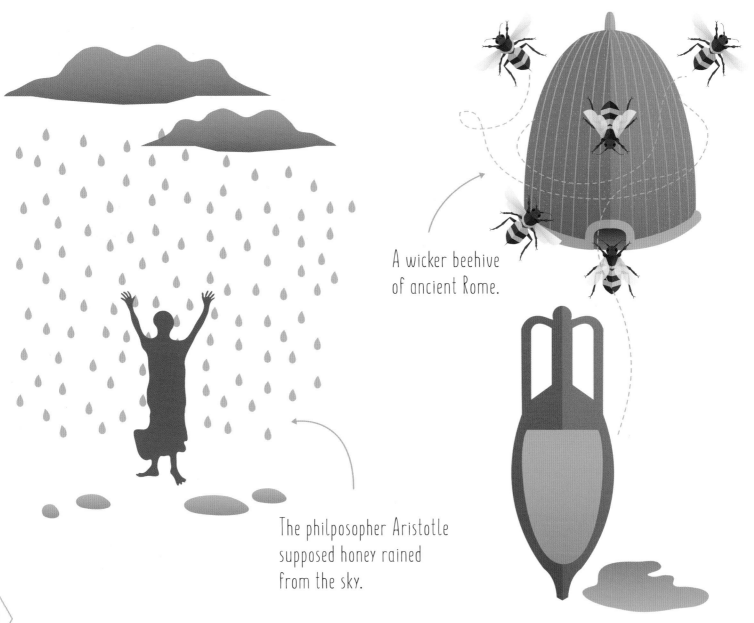

A wicker beehive of ancient Rome.

The philposopher Aristotle supposed honey rained from the sky.

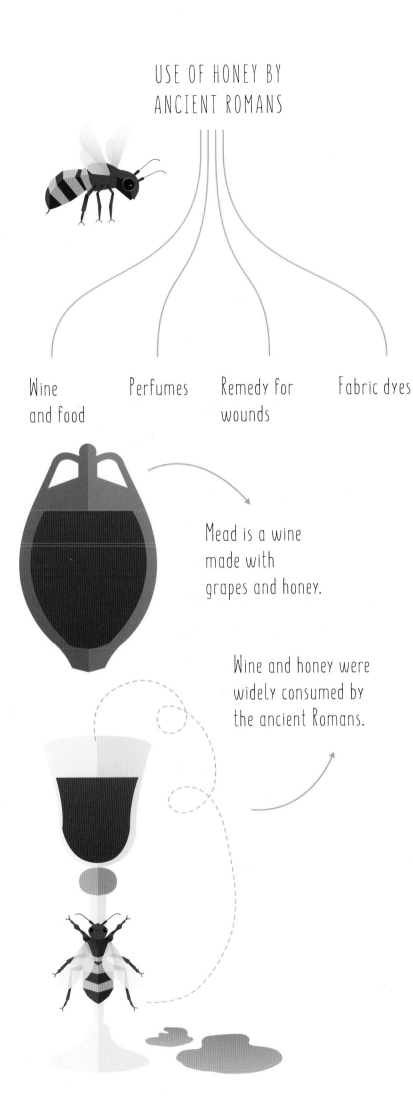

USE OF HONEY BY ANCIENT ROMANS

Wine and food

Perfumes

Remedy for wounds

Fabric dyes

Mead is a wine made with grapes and honey.

Wine and honey were widely consumed by the ancient Romans.

HONEY IN THE MIDDLE AGES

In the Middle Ages, with an edict proclaimed in the year 759, Charlesmagne obliged all his subjects to raise bees in every farm, in order to make honey and mead, a wine enriched with honey already well-known in Roman times, which became one of the most popular beverages in that period.

Thanks to the careful work of monks, abbeys and monasteries became the ideal places for experimenting new beekeeping techniques.

HONEY IN THE ARABIC WORLD

The Islamic world considered honey a divine food, and it is interesting to notice that the characteristic desserts of Northern Europe, made with spices and honey, have actually Middle-Eastern origins: the recipes imported from the crusaders returning from the Holy Land.

North European desserts made with honey come from the Arabic world.

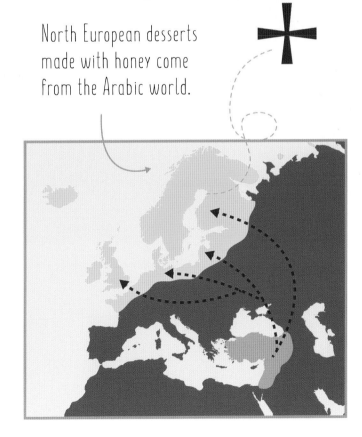

HONEY DURING THE RENAISSANCE

With the Renaissance, honey made its way peremptorily into kitchens, with the creation of dishes that were spectacular in taste and color and meant to surprise guests. It is at the end of this period that the custom of serving dessert at the end of the meal, still practiced today, began. Honey was still greatly used in preparing medications.

Rice and honey cake was a popular dessert during the Renaissance.

The chestnut flower

THE ADVENT OF SUGAR

Starting from 1600, though, the cultivation of sugarcane on tropical islands and of sugar beets in Europe became ever more widespread, so that sugar became more popular than honey.

And yet, fortunately, beekeeping wasn't abandoned, rather the contrary: new inventions, such as the honey extractor, made it possible to obtain honey that was purer and free of substances capable of altering its flavor.

Despite the advent of sugar, beekeeping continued to progress.

DIFFERENT HONEY FROM DIFFERENT FLOWERS

It was only at the start of the last century, though, that it became clear how honey was closely connected to the species of plant from which the pollen used by the bees came from, and so, in the 70s, began the production of honey derived from the pollen of one sole plant species (e.g. chestnut honey, tilia honey, etc.), with specific characteristics and taste.

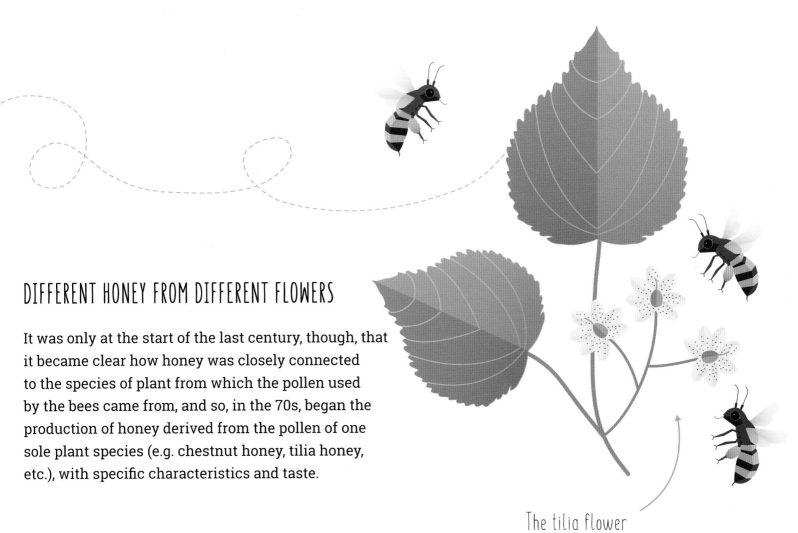

The tilia flower

Polyflower honey is made from the pollen of many different types of flowers.

HONEY TODAY

Today honey is rightly advertised as a food that's healthy, easy to digest, appropriate for everyone, particularly children and the elderly, and its consumption ought to be promoted.

16. BETWEEN SPIRITUALITY AND SYMBOLISM

In the course of history and at every corner of the earth, the various populations have always considered animals as symbols; they were useful in impersonating qualities or traits of human beings and their deities: the bee was no exception. This small insect has almost always been seen as a positive animal symbol, the representation of industriousness and spirit of cooperation, an example from which men could learn nothing but proper behavior.

ANCIENT EGYPT: DIVINE BEINGS

In ancient Egypt the bee was considered a divine being, since it was born from a tear of Ra, the sun god; it was associated with the soul and it was believed that it had the power to bring the dead back to life if it entered the deceased person's mouth.

ANCIENT GREECE: COLOR OF GOLD

The ancient Greeks would tell the legends of Zeus, nurtured as a child with a special honey made by bees of the island of Crete; to thank them, once grown up, the father of the gods supposedly gave them their color, that recalls the glitter of gold.

RA, the sun god

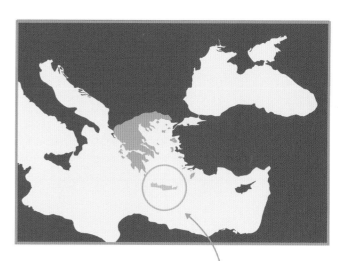

The island of Crete

ANCIENT ROME: SACRED MESSENGERS

Bees were considered by the Romans sacred messengers sent by Jupiter on the earth to carry up in the sky the prayers of men.

They were also considered carriers of divine knowledge: for babies visited in their crib by bees was predicted great fame as orators, just as, according to legend, happened to the great Greek philosopher Plato and to the Latin poet Virgil.

Ignoring the various stages of their life cycle, Greeks and Romans believed that bees originated from the skin of animals killed during sacrifice rituals to the gods. This is the reason why they symbolized the returning to life and immortality of the soul; furthermore, it was common belief that the dead that had led an honest life returned on the earth in the form of bees.

For the ancient Romans, bees were carriers of prophecies and messengers of the gods.

For Greeks and Romans, bees represented the immortality of the soul.

CHRISTIANITY: A SPIRITUAL MODEL

Christianity picked up most of these traditions, attributing to the bee, which was considered free of vice, high values of industriousness, purity, chastity and wisdom.

According to a legend, something extraordinary happened to St. Rita da Cascia when she was a baby: while she was sleeping in a basket placed on the floor, a swarm of bees alighted on her face without doing her the least harm. Her parents took it as a sign of God announcing the future greatness of their daughter.

Thanks to St. Ambrose, the beehive was taken as model of the structure of the Church: inside, the devout (that is, the bees) find refuge, protection, food, help and tranquility. Also, the belief that the bee fed only on the scent of flowers led St. Bernard of Chiaravalle to propound it as a symbol of great purity, therefore worthy of symbolizing the Holy Ghost.

Diametrically opposed to the bee, a divine symbol, was the fly, a demonic animal associated with the worst evils.

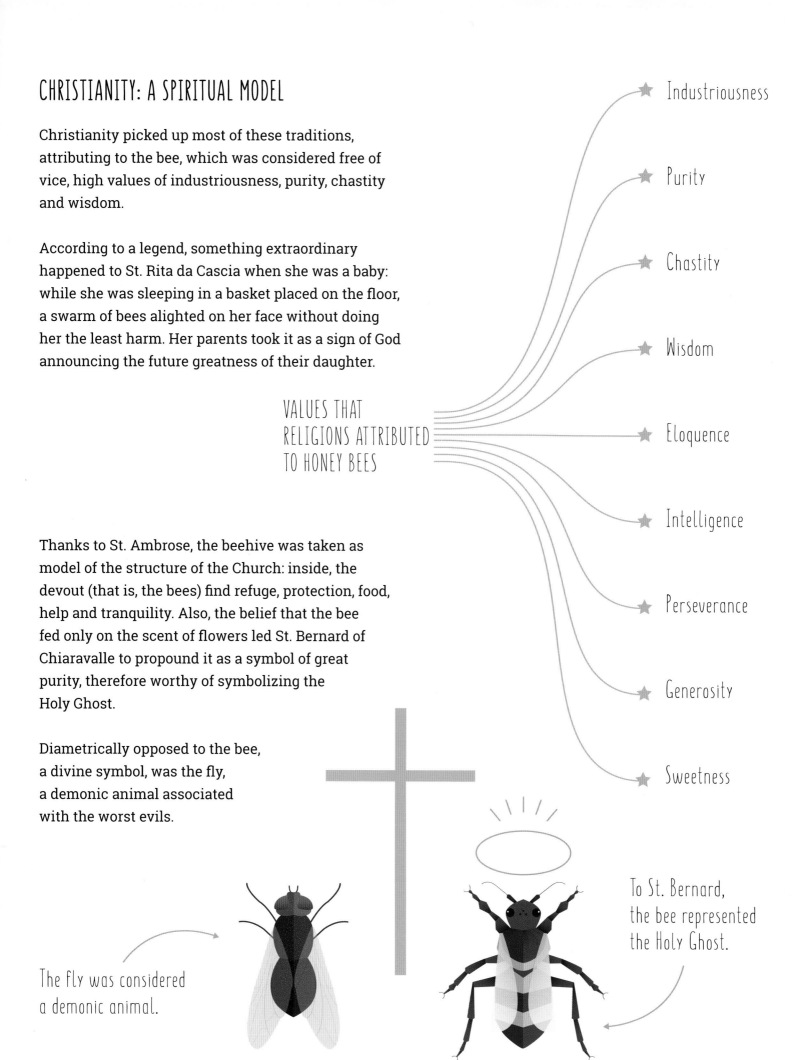

VALUES THAT RELIGIONS ATTRIBUTED TO HONEY BEES

- Industriousness
- Purity
- Chastity
- Wisdom
- Eloquence
- Intelligence
- Perseverance
- Generosity
- Sweetness

The fly was considered a demonic animal.

To St. Bernard, the bee represented the Holy Ghost.

JUDAISM

But other religions as well adopted the bee as a positive model: in Judaism, for example, it was associated with language, and so represented eloquence and intelligence. It is therefore connected to thought, the activity that distinguishes man from other animals and brings him closer to God.

Of the various bee products, wax too was highly valued for making candles to dedicate to God. Also, Jewish doctrine describes the Promised Land as a paradise on earth, the place where flows milk and honey.

ISLAM

As in the case of other cultures and religions, even for Islam the bee has been a symbol of perseverance, industriousness and intelligence, but also of grace and femininity. Furthermore, by giving honey to man, it symbolizes generosity and sweetness. For these devout followers, the soul leaves the body in the form of a bee and flies circling around the tomb of the deceased for 40 days, after which it can find a place in the sky.

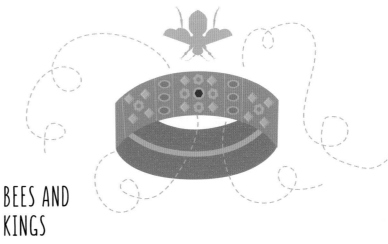

BEES AND KINGS

The bee and the hive represent an example of virtue even in the political sphere. Many nations with a king in charge made it their symbol so as to indicate the close resemblance between the two organizations: just as in the beehive only one rules, the queen bee, and the fate of the entire colony depends on her, so it must be in the Ideal State governed by a king, an emperor or a pope. For this reason many royal families have included bees in their family crest.

Moreover, bees represent virtues that make a people great: obedience to laws and authority, industriousness and honesty, justice, proper management of economic resources, well-being.

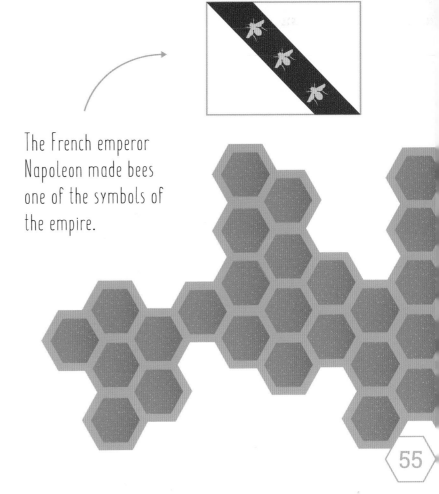

The French emperor Napoleon made bees one of the symbols of the empire.

17. THE GREAT BEE FAMILY

Bees, either domesticated or wild, solitary or with a social life, all belong to the same family, the Apidae, that groups about 20,000 species. Of all these species, only 5% live in a community, while the remaining 95% is represented by solitary bees.

1 Among social bees, besides the well-known honey bees, there are the bumble bees (e.g. *Bombus*), easily recognizable by their round and furry body. Bumble

2 bees form small colonies made up averagely by about fifty individuals, but can reach up to 300. The colonies do not last long: no more than one season.

5%
ARE SOCIAL BEES

1
HONEY BEE

2
BUMBLE BEE

3
MELIPONINE

4
CUCKOO BEE

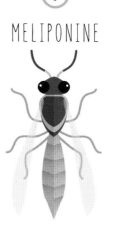

3 Some species of the Apidae family are armed with a stinger and equipped with venom, while others lack these completely, or have such a short stinger that they are unable to use it.

An example of these are meliponines, tropical bees that have social behavior and are raised for honey too, that do not possess stingers and defend themselves by biting.

THE GREAT APIDAE FAMILY
INCLUDES **20,000** SPECIES

(5) Slightly less popular, the Euglossine or orchid bees have a characteristic metallic coloration. The males, thanks to special structures on their legs, gather the scent of flowers that, apparently, serves to attract a female companion. This habit makes them very useful for pollination, particularly that of orchids. Despite being solitary bees, cooperation may occur between females that build their nests next to each other inside a log or between the roots of a tree.

(4) As for solitary bees, each female must provide alone for its brood, building a nest for each egg. Some species, such as the Nomadinae, also called cuckoo bees, just like the birds who parasitize the nests of other birds, they use the nest of other Apidae, without going through the trouble of building one of their own: once found an unguarded nest, they deposit an egg in it, using its shelter and food for the young larva.
Once it is born, it quickly gets rid of its host's brood and enjoys the nest all for itself.

95%
ARE SOLITARY BEES

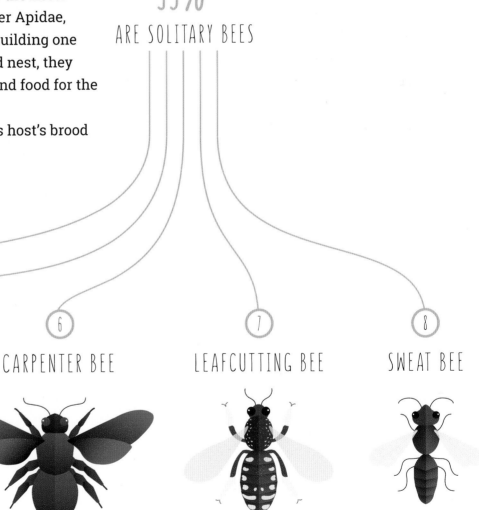

(5) ORCHID BEE   (6) CARPENTER BEE   (7) LEAFCUTTING BEE   (8) SWEAT BEE

(6) (7) Among the more skillful nest-builders are the carpenter bees (or *Xylocopine*), large and purplish black in color, and the leafcutting bees (or *Megachillidae*), capable of cutting out circular pieces of leaves and petals with which they fill the cells of the nest destined to contain the eggs.

(8) Finally, though a bit odd, but nonetheless interesting, there are the Halictidae or sweat bees, which are attracted by precisely this odoriferous secretion.

18. ARE BEES DISAPPEARING?

In recent years we have been witnessing a worrisome phenomenon that presently seems relentless: the number of bees, in particular honey bees, is decreasing just about all over the world. According to data of the environmental organization GREEPEACE, in Europe the loss in recent years has been 53%, while beekeepers in some areas of the United States report that it has reached 90% in only one year! This should sound a warning bell.

A PLANET THAT RISKS WITHERING

On top of all this, we must add the consequent extinction of thousands of wild flowering plants that, for many, results in a catastrophic prediction: in a few years the earth's biodiversity would be at risk, with unimaginable damage to the entire biosphere.

DAMAGE TO AGRICULTURE

As is common knowledge, in fact, bees are extremely useful insects, not only for the production of honey, but for plant pollination as well; with their decrease in number, crop yield plummets and the economic damage to farmers is inestimable. In fact, we must consider that, of the 100 plant species providing 90% of the world population's food production, over 75% are pollinated by bees.

WHAT DO WE KNOW?

The problem, therefore, is getting serious and, for this reason, scientists are conducting research in the attempt to understand its causes and find a solution.

The phenomenon is known as Colony Collapse Disorder (CCD).

What has been discovered so far? What are the causes? Presently we are only capable of drawing up hypotheses.

19. UNDERSTANDING THE PROBLEM

MALNUTRITION AND UNDERNOURISHMENT

In areas where monoculture is practiced (that is, one type of crop grown on very vast croplands), bees have only one type of nectar available, and their diet would seem to be less balanced and complete. This would lower their resistance to disease.

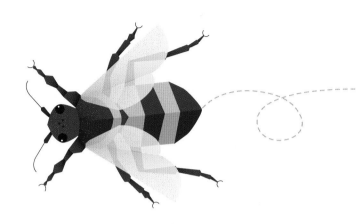

INSECTICIDES AND PESTICIDES

Insecticides such as neonicotinoids and toxic substances used in agriculture, particularly the excessive use of these substances in intensive farming, threatens directly the life of bees or contaminates the pollen that the bees gather and take into the hive.

EPIDEMICS

Lately, there has been an outspread of parasites, such as *Varroa destructor*, a parasitic species of mite that arrived in Europe from Asia in the 80s and that feeds on the blood of bees, weakening their immune system. An entire beehive infested with *Varroa* mites dies in little time.

INCREASE IN CROP CULTIVATION

It necessarily leads to a reduction or fragmentation of natural or semi-natural ecosystems, such as woods, hedges and meadows, that represent important sources of nectar.

ELECTROMAGNETIC FIELDS

According to some German researchers, the electromagnetic waves generated by cell phones reduce bees' perception of the Earth's magnetic field, thus causing them to lose their sense of direction.

CLIMATIC CHANGE

They involve, though very gradually, changes in the weather by increasing the periods of rain and extending those of drought. In both cases, the number of days available to bees for gathering nectar and pollen decreases. This way, an environment turns into a place in which bees can no longer thrive.

WHAT CAN WE DO?

To limit this phenomenon before it's too late, it would suffice if all the countries in the world came to an agreement and implemented some good practices, starting from simple operations focused on preserving natural habitats, reducing the use of pesticides in agriculture and banning the more toxic ones, and supporting scientific research on the phenomenon.

But each one of us can do a little something to help save the bees: let's grow on our balconies some nutritious and very relished flowers for these useful insects.

LIST OF THE BEES ENCOUNTERED IN THIS BOOK

HONEY BEE

ORCHID BEE

VIOLET CARPENTER
BEE

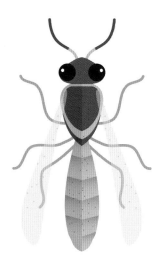

MELIPONINE

SWEAT BEE

BUILDER BEE

MINING BEE

BUMBLE BEE

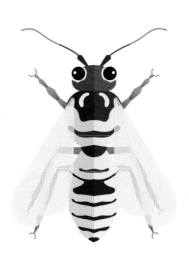

CUCKOO BEE

CARPENTER BEE

LEAFCUTTING BEE

Cristina Banfi

A graduate in Natural Sciences at the Università degli Studi di Milano, she has taught in various schools. She is a founding partner of Associazione Didattica Museale (ADM) and ADMaiora, organizations involved in teaching in museums and at exhibits. For more than 20 years now she has been working in the field of scientific communication and teaching through play and can boast several publications for both classroom and general education purposes, particularly for audiences of children and teenagers. In recent years she has written several books for White Star Kids.

The Museum Teaching Association (Associazione Didattica Museale)

Founded in 1994, the organization has been active for more than 20 years in the field of education; it manages the Educational Services of important museums, such as the City Museum of Natural History in Milan, Genoa, Novara and Trieste, besides being involved with teaching in sanctuaries and natural parks, both publicly and privately owned.

Giulia De Amicis

Born in Milan in 1986, after earning her master's degree in Design she started to work as information designer and illustrator for small studios, newspapers, and ENGOs. Through the years she has studied and lived in Italy, Spain, India and Greece. Presently she lives and works in Brighton, England. In the past years she has realized several books for White Star Publishers.

Graphic Design
Valentina Figus

WSKids
WHITE STAR KIDS

White Star Kids® is a registered trademark property of White Star s.r.l.

© 2018 White Star s.r.l.
Piazzale Luigi Cadorna, 6 – 20123 Milan, Italy
www.whitestar.it

Translation: Ellisse s.a.s. of Sergio Abate & C.

ISBN 978-88-544-1276-7
2 3 4 5 6   23 22 21 20 19

Printed in Italia by Rotolito S.p.A. – Seggiano di Pioltello (Milan)